Mastering

THE ART OF SUBSTITUTE TEACHING

by
S. HAROLD COLLINS
designed & illustrated by
GARY J. SCHUBERT

Published by:
Garlic Press
605 Powers
Eugene, OR 97402

www.garlicpress.com

Preface

Only in the past few years have teaching materials been published which focus on substitute teaching. Most of these materials have divided their offerings into lessons according to subject matter areas — lessons for math, for language arts, for science, etc. While these offerings are good, little if nothing has been published which attempts to carry substitute teaching beyond segmented presentations and to establish a broader teaching format from which to teach as a Substitute Teacher. This book suggests a broad teaching format.

The success of the format relies heavily upon planning. Yes, Substitute Teachers must plan subject matter presentations, but a planning as equally weighted must be devoted to several other factors. Substitute Teachers must plan — in the sense of develop — techniques which deal effectively and immediately with student behavior. And Substitute Teachers must communicate a style and personality which quickly gains the confidence and the cooperation of the students they encounter.

Within the suggested format, I have written much of my own substitute teaching style and personality. I have done so with the hope that my experiences, techniques, and methods will provide you either a basis or a spark for your own substitute teaching.

Table of Contents

The Changing Role of the Substitute Teacher

1

Substitute teaching has long been a neglected teaching role, having been undermined by too many negative connotations. Regular classroom teachers too often regard Substitute Teachers as mere babysitters, while administrators are too often more concerned with simply getting *some body* to fill an absent teacher's position than with placing a qualified Substitute Teacher. And even Substitute Teachers, made embarrassingly aware of these attitudes held by their peers, too often fail to regard themselves as legitimate and necessary teachers in the conduct of daily education.

These negative connotations, however, are changing in such a fashion as to distinguish the role of the Substitute Teacher and to benefit the course of overall education. In the front of this change is the type of teaching professional assuming the position. In past years, Substitute Teachers were recruited largely from the ranks of older teaching professionals and from teachers, largely women, who wanted only an occasional or a limited contact with the classroom. These professionals whose lives, finances, and family commitments allowed them intermittent contact with the classroom found the part-time nature of substitute teaching desirable.

In recent years, however, substitute teaching has attracted a greater, and a generally younger, variety of teaching professional, owing to the competition for regular classroom positions. The reduced number of school age children has been reflected in a corresponding reduction in demand for teachers. Many teachers, particularly those newly trained, have turned to substitute teaching as an alternative to a regular classroom position. They have done so largely with the hope that both substitute teaching experience and classroom exposure will provide a foot in the door to a full-time, contracted position.

With a substantial change in the type, quality, and number of teachers turning to substitute teaching as a viable teaching situation, there is a clear need for the educational community to channel this teaching potential to benefit the classroom. Channeling this potential requires a cooperative effort. Teacher training institutions must begin to include specific training for the substitute teaching situation, while school districts must attend more closely to the specialized needs and uniquenesses of substitute teaching. Administrators must look to Substitute Teachers as more than a *replacement* who will keep the lid on for a day or two. And regular classroom teachers must prepare their students to accept Substitute Teachers as a natural part of the educational process.

The Myth

3

A certain myth constantly emanates from the ranks of Substitute Teachers: *"Substitute Teachers have it the worst."* An often self-fulfilling prophecy, this belief distorts two common teaching conditions: the seemingly constant experiencing of behavior problems by Substitute Teachers, and the lack of information and peer support provided Substitute Teachers as they daily assume new classroom situations.

Student behavior is a challenge to all educators and not just of special concern to Substitute Teachers. Regular classroom teachers have, admittedly, an advantage in being able to deal with inappropriate or distractive behavior over a longer period of time. But inappropriate or distractive behavior poses many of the same periods of frustration, wheel spinning, or *fire suppression* for the regular classroom teacher as it does for the Substitute Teacher. Substitute Teachers must consciously use and develop techniques that check, head off, or solve problems which allow behavior to disrupt the classroom. Behavior problems are a given and complaint or inattention serves only to evade a personal resolve to deal with such problems.

The myth also implies a second classroom condition which of its very nature often distracts Substitute Teachers from dealing with it fully. The perspective and support, as reflected by background information and school policies, that is extended to Substitute Teachers in daily assignments is too often sketchy or non-existent. Substitute Teachers deserve a clear picture of their teaching assignments: the behavior of the students, the methods and expectations of the regular classroom teacher, pertinent background as related to subject matter, lesson plans for the immediate day, and definitive statements of administrative support. As with behavior problems, Substitute Teachers must exercise a personal resolve to handle these matters whether through development of specialized techniques or open inquiry.

Substitute Teachers need to eliminate the myth of themselves as *burdened educators*. They must, individually, at least in the early stages, accept a responsibility to deal directly with student behavior and the lack of classroom information and peer support. When regular classroom teachers, administrators, and other school members begin to deal with these problems too, providing assistance to the already Substitute Teacher initiated efforts, the myth will have vanished, and a greater teaching continuity will exist within schools.

More Than Just Surviving

Substitute Teachers must be prepared to meet a wide variety of classroom situations, contend with a diversity of student attitudes, and heed established school and district policies. Such situations, attitudes, and policies can change radically from one day to the next. Being able to accommodate such a variety of circumstances typifies the substitute teaching role.

Yet it is very easy for Substitute Teachers, knowing they probably will not return to the same assignment tomorrow, to view their teaching assignments as separate, day-to-day experiences. This separate, day-to-day attitude is especially clear when things do not go well. Then it becomes very easy to reduce the experience to a survival level, *"If I can get through today, all will be well. The regular teacher will return tomorrow, anyway."*

Separate experiences of *just surviving* are very shortsighted commitments to substitute teaching. Each confines and limits the teaching experience to episodes that have no overall continuity. To more than just survive and to regard substitute teaching as more than separate, unrelated experiences, a Substitute Teacher should examine his or her relationship to the classroom: How can (s)he affect classroom learning? What influence can student behavior have on Substitute Teacher behavior? How does a Substitute Teacher take charge in a classroom?

4

How Substitute Teachers Affect Learning

Substitute teaching assignments are, generally, for short periods. How, in short time spans, can a Substitute Teacher expect to influence learning? Are there any means that will decisively measure to what extent a Substitute Teacher has affected learning during his/her brief classroom stay? No, there are not. Then, perhaps a Substitute Teacher is justified simply to babysit a classroom or to keep the lid on. No, again.

Substitute Teachers have two distinct capabilities which can influence student learning. One allows Substitute Teachers to reinforce skills that are characteristic to a grade level. Reinforcing skills requires Substitute Teachers to prepare lessons and materials which are appropriate.

The second capability is very subtle. Substitute Teachers have a unique chance to influence student self-concepts. New people can possess an attractive aura for students. And this aura can serve to engage students in learning that may not have, in past experiences, been altogether productive or positive. The aura effect is nothing mystical. It is simply a tool to establish a quick communication channel with students, getting them first to listen and then to perform. The more or greater success that students gain from performance, the better will be their concepts of themselves as functioning, capable people.

Providing a different opportunity for students to experience successful learning is important. It carries responsibilities, too. Substitute Teachers must prepare their content presentations and they must give positive-directive feedback in their interactions with students.

Classroom Behavior

The student and the Substitute Teacher

Dealing with student behavior is a major classroom challenge. In a substitute teaching situation it can be devastating, reducing the best of teaching intentions to frustration, anger, and ultimately to just surviving for that day. Substitute Teachers must be able to handle inappropriate or distractive student behavior as it affects classroom learning and as it affects their own teaching composure.

The time worn motto *Be Prepared* serves well for Substitute Teachers. The better prepared a Substitute Teacher is with engaging and interesting lessons, facts, and materials, the more attentive — and conversely, the less distractive — students will generally be. The more involved students are with a Substitute Teacher, the less energy they will devote to misbehavior.

In addition to subject matter presentations, Substitute Teachers must develop an ability to appraise the goals that students express through their behavior. Behavior is purposeful. The difficulty lies in determining the purpose for which behavior is enacted and then dealing with that behavior in a positive manner. This requires sensitive observations and equally sensitive responses.

Considerable student behavior, the behavior which Substitute Teachers experience the most, centers about the desire for attention and the desire to exert power. A student's desire for attention is expressed in countless ways — talking out, falling out of a chair, asking repeated questions, wild tales, repeated need for help, cuteness, charm, throwing things, restlessness, and other minor mischief. The Substitute Teacher who is able to perceive these types of mechanisms as attention-getters is better able to deal with them, while not succumbing to feelings of frustration or annoyance.

The Substitute Teacher who becomes annoyed or frustrated in dealing with misbehavior and who tries to enforce conformity is easily pushed into a contest for power. A student or an entire class may become aggressive, wantonly disregarding order and discipline. Power struggles are devastating, since they cut quickly to the ego, challenging teacher authority and worthiness. Kids have an extremely effective way of *winning out* in struggle situations. Substitute Teachers must be able to recognize the warning signs of a pending power struggle and endeavor to keep their sails out of any such mounting winds.

Substitute Teachers not only must develop an ability to recognize patterns of student behavior, but they must also develop an awareness of how such behavior can involve their own personal responses. Children are very quick to recognize how teachers respond to behavior. They are very quick to recognize that they can activate certain teacher responses, like buttons, at will. And they will delight in activating these buttons — anger, frustration, love, acceptance, pity — with remarkable success, time after time after time unless Substitute Teachers recognize that their own responses to certain behavior may in fact contribute to that very behavior.

If a student is constantly disruptive in class, the Substitute Teacher must maintain a personal awareness of how that behavior influences his or her own composure and mood. A problem exists with the child's behavior and that behavior must not trigger anger, frustration, or other Substitute Teacher responses that will complicate the situation. Being aware of one's own personal behavior does not warrant a facade of callousness or aloofness to eliminate vulnerability, but it does allow for responses that are neither baited nor reflexive.

6

Taking Charge in the Classroom

The first few minutes in a new teaching assignment are especially important for a Substitute Teacher. In this short time, (s)he must quickly satisfy a number of procedural demands: lunch count, attendance, flag salute, introduce him or herself, explain what knowledge (s)he may or may not have about the absent teacher, and confidently take charge of the class to present a meaningful day. *Taking charge* not only includes the presentation of subject matter lessons, but most importantly, it clearly establishes what expectations, rules, and limits will be observed during the conduct of the day.

Establishing expectations, rules, and limits can be done exclusively by the Substitute Teacher, it can be done by convincing students that the expectations, rules, and limits are for their own good, or it can be done by concluding an agreement with the students. All methods have a place.

How a Substitute Teacher handles routine start-of-the-day matters while interacting with the class will prove a significant indication of how the entire day will proceed. This is the time when students will be the most attentive to what the Substitute Teacher has to offer. A laissez-faire attitude by the Substitute Teacher toward the students and toward his or her own goals for the day will too easily lead to an unproductive and chaotic day. A deliberate approach is imperative.

Preparing To Teach

Substitute Teachers must be prepared to teach on their own. They can not rely wholly on the absent teacher's preparation. Their lessons must be relevant and they must develop techniques which lead to a successful student-Substitute Teacher relationship.

Access to and knowledge of teaching resources is a must. Sources for ideas and assistance must be constantly developed by each Substitute Teacher. School districts, by in large, do not provide Substitute Teachers with a comprehensive knowledge of available district or commercial resources appropriate to substitute teaching. Nor, again do they routinely make available to Substitute Teachers the assistance, materials, and supplies that are provided regular staff members. Until Substitute Teachers achieve or are granted the status of bona fide *staff* members, a recognition which opens a wider availability to teaching resources, they must satisfy themselves to pursue classroom preparation unassisted.

Lesson preparation must not only cover a wide range of grades, a wide range of subjects, and a wide range of classroom teaching approaches (accommodating the open classroom or the traditional classroom), but it must produce quick results. Substitute teaching assignments are, characteristically, one or two days in length. The length of these assignments does not allow for long, protacted involvement.

What sources are available for lesson planning? Professional magazines, which may often be found in faculty rooms, provide or suggest lesson ideas.

The classroom is a many faceted resource for ideas. Ideas that the regular classroom teacher has developed whether through displays, bulletin boards, worksheets, or student projects are ready sources.

School districts often publish manuals or materials that are available to regular staff members. Substitute Teachers should use these materials and insist on their being provided all substitute teachers on a regular basis. Such insistence will make important materials available and will inform the school district of Substitute Teacher needs. Many school districts have curriculum libraries; sometimes curriculum libraries are provided on a county basis.

Stores catering solely to teachers and teaching materials are a recent phenomenon. In the past, catalogue orders were the main source of commercially produced teaching materials; now, small concerns which carry a diversity of teaching products are becoming commonplace. These stores can provide selected resources appropriate for substitute teaching.

For further assistance, see the selected bibliography at the end of this book. In it are listed selected professional articles and commercial products which have specific use for Substitute Teachers.

8

Whose Lessons?

Substitute Teachers must gather their own materials and prepare their own lessons. They must be prepared to teach from their own plans when the plans of the regular classroom teacher are not available, sketchy, or incomprehensible. Some teachers are very thorough in planning, others express their plans in brief phrases or key words understandable only to themselves. Even in the event of an illness or an emergency leave, some teachers will annotate plans and somehow — through a friend or relative — make sure those plans arrive in the classroom. If a Substitute Teacher is prepared to teach and if plans, in whatever state of refinement, are present in a classroom, whose plans have priority?

Substitute Teachers must exercise keen discrimination regarding the most appropriate plans. Should a teacher's plans be followed exactly? How descript are the teacher's plans? How comfortable is the Substitute Teacher with the subject matter? Will the regular classroom teacher need to undo any of the Substitute Teacher's work? These are questions that require immediate Substitute Teacher consideration.

If an absent teacher indicates that a Substitute Teacher may, as (s)he sees fit, present his or her own plans, the Substitute Teacher has a certain latitude. But in the many instances when the latitude is not provided, Substitute Teachers must be careful in their selection of plans. A regular classroom should expect a certain compliance with their lesson planning.

Strategies for Teaching

There are three strategies that a Substitute Teacher can use to conduct a teaching day — actually two, with the third being a combination of the first two: (1) a Substitute Teacher can follow the plans of the regular classroom teacher, expanding upon those plans to teach points that the teacher has indicated; (2) a Substitute Teacher can teach from her or his own prepared lessons; or (3) a Substitute Teacher can teach from both the plans of the regular classroom teacher and his or her own plans.

Teaching from someone else's plans is difficult. This strategy, relying upon the presence of plans, requires an ability to step into the midst of student learning and to continue much as the regular classroom teacher would. It often presupposes that the Substitute Teacher knows what has taken place and how her or his immediate part contributes to tomorrow's sequence. This strategy also requires an ability to expand the plans to get at what the absent teacher desires. Expanding is particularly important if plans are generally stated: ''Read and discuss pages 125 - 142''; or, ''Have the students write a creative composition about frogs''; or ''Help the class review for their test tomorrow.'' The techniques that a Substitute Teacher uses to discuss a topic, to spark a creative assignment about a potentially dull theme, or to review material about which the class probably has a greater knowledge than the Substitute Teacher are crucial to the success of this strategy.

Teaching from one's own planning is quite the opposite of teaching from what an absent teacher has planned. A Substitute Teacher is most acquainted and most secure dealing with what (s)he has created. The aura of a new person and his/her manner of presentation are positive factors to the success of this strategy.

A strategy that incorporates both of the preceding approaches balances the absent teacher's necessities and the Substitute Teacher's variations. Which of these three strategies is to be used is a judgment that a Substitute Teacher must make after considering the numerous factors that immediately influence his/her assignment.

10

Notes on this section . . . .

Introductions

How a morning begins, or how a class period begins, largely sets the tone for what is to follow throughout the day. Your attentiveness to these first few minutes serves to establish so much.

You have two choices. You can allow the students to begin the motion of the day, with you reacting accordingly. Or you can begin the motion of the day, getting the kids involved. The first choice, although it may sound *free*, is too often a losing choice for a Substitute Teacher. Students have their expectations of Substitute Teachers and they have been allowed by teachers and administrators — and Substitute Teachers for that matter — to regard Substitute Teachers as *fair game* for pranks and inappropriate behavior (this attitude needs to be addressed by all concerned). Unless the school environment is one which places significant emphasis on student responsibility and is one in which Substitute Teachers are a fully integrated part of the teaching staff, allowing students to take the opening lead places the Substitute Teacher in a catch-up role, constantly putting out small, distractive fires while major control eludes containment.

The Substitute Teacher who sets the direction of the morning and who takes charge from the beginning provides the classroom experience of that day with the best chance for success. In accomplishing this feat, you must give the kids a sense of who you are, what expectations you have, and what the mood of the day can be.

You must realize that your presence in a new classroom is a big plus for you. The kids do not know who you are. They can not tag you immediately. They have nothing to grasp onto, until you begin your — hopefully planned — opening statements, remarks, and gestures.

So . . . if you have the stage and an attentive audience, how do you begin? And as the day unfolds, how do you make transitions into subject matter areas?

No matter what clamor or uproar proceeds the official beginning of the class, your initial request for attention is going to be heeded (*is going to be* sounds pretty positive, which is what you have to be!!). This is one moment or time span that the kids are going to be very attentive, their attentiveness is directed at clues which reveal just who you are and what you are. You have a chance to provide students with information that they need to know, to gather information that you need to know, and to establish expectations for the day. The entire process requires the most positive, engaging techniques that you have.

Kids need certain facts. What happened to the regular teacher? Who are you? What do you expect of them? What are you like? Will anything different happen today?

You need certain facts. Is there a lunch count? A flag salute? Special opening procedures? Are there things that the kids want to tell you concerning the conduct of a normal day?

You will need to develop a patter that will make key statements to the kids, such as: "I need your help (enlist help)." "I expect certain things, they are . . . . . ." "I'm not like Ms./Mr. _____, I don't do everything like (s)he does." "Let me tell you about myself . . . . . ." "I have some things that I have brought with me today that I think you will enjoy (build expectations)."

You will need to include probing questions which draw out facts, revealing how a normal day proceeds and how the regular teacher performs.

Here is a patter that might serve as an example. It is my standard opener — like anything that will be presented in this book, my approaches are not gospel, they are only suggestions to be revamped as your own person finds fitting, or to be spin-offs for yet other approaches:

(Bell) I would like everyone's attention up here. (Pause) Thank you.

My name is _____ (first name, last name, or both). I don't exactly know what happened to Ms./Mr. _____. But I'm here for the day and I'm looking forward to an interesting time. I've brought some things that can make our time a bit different. But it all depends on you. If I can get your help and cooperation, things should be a bit different today. And I think you will enjoy yourselves.

Can someone tell me, by raising a hand, about lunch count, duties, schedules (etc.). Thank you for raising your hand. (Get whatever bits you need and move on.)

There are a few things I want to tell you about myself. I expect . . . . . . I'm a happy person and I like to stay that way. But I can be mean and nasty, pull my hair, stamp my feet, and shout if I must.

This opener can be precise and quick or it can be interspersed with student responses. In any case, you are presenting yourself, and however you do it, the kids are getting to know you.

Move on to a quick activity that involves the class. An activity at this point, while possibly just for effect, provides important two-way communication; the kids gain more about you, and you begin to gather information about their maturity, standards, behavior, etc. The interactions that the following 'Introduction' activities foster are crucial to Substitute Teacher-student rapport.

14

Name Game

Names are special possessions. Knowing someone's name supposes a familiarity with that person. When a Substitute Teacher knows a student's name, there can be a certain positive link between the two.

For a Substitute Teacher to enter a classroom and to know the names of the kids — or at least the kids believe the Substitute Teacher knows specific names — is a definite advantage. I am terrible with names, I often call roll from first names, so — as I tell the kids — I can associate a name and a face and won't have to go around all day saying, "Hey, you." I forget most of the names at once, but the kids have given me something that they believe I am capable of retaining. And, they have begun to disclose their individuality, their personal selves to me, just through the utterance of a first name.

The disclosure of names seems to strip away some of the ambiguity presented by new faces, new surroundings, and new attitudes that Substitute

Teachers continually meet. One game that serves to disclose names involves humor and enjoyment (*never* forget these qualities).

I explain that we are going to do something that will give me a chance (succor their help whenever possible) to learn their names. I begin by saying, "My name is Mr. Collins, I come from Kalamazoo on a kangaroo (to be more familiar, 'My name is Stan, I come from Siberia on a sheet.')"

After emphasizing the alliteration of name, place, and object, I then ask a volunteer to continue. Or, I start in an orderly fashion and proceed down rows.

Any response I make to an individual effort underscores recognition of the student's name and the student's alliterative effort. The combination of student-Substitute Teacher participation, enjoyment, and humor serves to establish a tone that can be further expanded throughout the day.

THE TWINS

Another Name Game

Depending upon how daring you are, you can either begin or end this *'Introduction.'* In any event the person starting states his/her name, "I'm Mr. Collins." The second person says, "I'm Chris and that is Mr. Collins." The sequence continues around the room with each person stating his/her name and repeating all of those names before him/her.

The activity is easy, of course, for the kids, they know one another. You will be surprised, too, at your ability to remember names, especially if you place yourself last and have to repeat everyone's name. If you are last, you can certainly play to the kids.

Variations of this Introduction add bits to the name, such as: something the student is good at, "I'm artistic Chris"; or, a descriptive adjective — in this example, a non-sense alliterative effort — "I'm crazy Chris."

What's in a Name

Another way to use names to establish student-Substitute Teacher rapport is by disclosing the origin of a child's name. Various resources provide an explanation of name origins. First names are best used for the classroom—there are more students with the first names of Jim and John, and Lori and Michelle than the last names of Cowsnowski, Hayakawa, or Devereaux.

I have a small, inexpensive paperback book that lists the origins of more than 600 popular first names. I tell of the book and express my willingness to look up the first name of a class member. The hands will immediately fly up, if not the voices sound. I take a few minutes to look up names, making brief, personal comments to the child after reading from the book.

You can not look up everyone's name. But several minutes spent attending to a few is time well spent. I usually leave the book in the front of the class somewhere, indicating that other interested students can come up during the day to find their names.

Names are prized possessions and everyone has a certain perception about his/her name. Kids especially, like the attention provided by the recognition of their name.

16

Who Is That Substitute Teacher?

From the moment students see that they have a Substitute Teacher, they begin to make judgments. Similarly, once the Substitute Teacher sees his or her charges, (s)he begins to make certain judgments, too. If (there are always qualifiers of which a perceptive Substitute Teacher must be aware) by my judgment I feel that the composure and maturity of the class can handle a specialized dialogue, I give the kids a chance to ask me questions.

Students can either raise their hands to ask a question, or they can write questions on a slip of paper to be handed in. Both methods have advantages. I have gone so far as to carry small slips of paper upon which there is a place for their name (anonymity sometimes encourages obnoxious writing) and three lines for questions.

The slip-of-paper method also occupies the students in a process of thought and writing, a period of time that allows me to get my bearings, especially if I need to take attendance or lunch count. The slip-of-paper method also allows me to censor or to tone down questions.

You must not be afraid of the questions kids will ask, some questions are quite personal. Kids are inquisitive. You have the chance while answering questions to speak to the child inquiring — by tone of voice, by eye contact, and with verbal praise. Answering questions is a good format to disclose yourself as a teacher, and more important, as a human being.

One class I taught was already familiar with this technique, but they performed it a bit differently. They placed me on a chair and then sat in a circle around me. They called it *Hot Seat*. They asked me questions such as: how old I was; what my marital status was; where I went to school; what sports I liked; what my family background was.

Great Masterpieces of Art

The Substitute Teacher as Entertainer

A little music,
A little dance,
A little seltzer down the pants.

The best received Introduction that I have ever performed is *Great Masterpieces of Art*. Great Masterpieces allows a Substitute Teacher to practice entertaining, to be an entertainer if you will.

"What! Education is not a show!" I can hear some say. Without realizing that entertainment is as much a part of teaching as it is of a full stage production, a Substitute Teacher (or any educator) misses a significant vehicle for learning and for personal happiness. Everyone needs to enjoy him or herself.

Here is a patter that introduces *Great Masterpieces of Art*:

> Whether you know it or not I collect great masterpieces of art. Over the years I have spent millions of dollars and traveled to far corners of the world to buy artwork.
>
> You're in luck today, because I have brought with me several masterpieces. And I'm going to show them to you.
>
> I'm sure you'll appreciate and probably recognize them right away. Remember, these are very old

Looking up a nose.

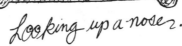

and they have cost me millions. Here is the first one . . . .

At that, I present a piece of colored posterboard that illustrates a nose (see illustration "Looking up a nose").

Mouths open, blank stares are apparent, finally giggles are heard, and someone says, "That's a masterpiece? What is it?"

I hope you recognize this as a Droodle. To the kids, I have built the whole presentation up, creating expectations, and all they have gotten is a figure that they could have reproduced by the time they were four years old.

Quickly the lightness of the activity is perceived; I continue:

> You don't recognize this? Hmm!
>
> Well, what do you think it is? I'm willing to listen to anyone who raises a hand and who thinks they have an idea. Be patient, I'll get around to everyone.

I always, with a betraying smile, insist that this is an expensive masterpiece for which I have traveled many miles. They know.

I usually have five or six masterpieces. They can all be shown at once. Or they can be shown at intervals. They are especially good for *Fillers* (see next section of this book) too. They can be used for an entire lesson later in the day, where the kids create their own masterpieces. There is incredible mileage — from variations — that this activity can provide.

Remember the entertainment quality that you, as a Substitute Teacher, can use to establish control, rapport, and enjoyment. Work on it!!

Stumpers

An *Introduction* technique that captures the attention of kids while simultaneously requiring them to assume a different perspective is the *Stumper*. A *Stumper* is:

■ How many animals of each species did Adam take aboard the ark with him?

■ If an international airliner crashed exactly on the U.S.-Canadian border, where would they be required to bury the survivors?

■ A farmer had 17 sheep. All but 9 died. How many did he have left?

■ An archeologist reported finding two gold coins dated 46 B.C. At a banquet honoring him, he was thoroughly discredited by an angry, fellow archeologist. Why?

■ If you went to bed at eight o'clock at night, and set your alarm to get up at nine o'clock in the morning, why on earth — after 13 hours of rest — are you so sleepy?

■ If your doctor gave you three pills and told you to take one every half hour, how long would be required to take all three pills?

■ How much dirt may be removed from a hole that is three feet deep, two feet wide, and ten feet long?

■ How many three cent stamps in a dozen?

■ A child is playing in the sand. (S)he has 6 ½ sandpiles in one place and 3 ½ in another. If (s)he puts them all together, how many sandpiles would (s)he have?

■ The Large family has seven girls and each girl has one brother. Including Mr. and Mrs. Large, how many are in the family?

■ If you drop a steel ball, would it fall more rapidly through water at 20 degrees or water at 60 degrees?

■ There are seven maple trees and on the seven maple trees are seven branches. On the seven branches are seven acorns. How many acorns are there altogether?

Place one or several of these stumpers on the front board for the kids to see as they come in. Use an appropriate interaction with the students to answer them.

19

Codes

Codes are another good way to capture the attention of students. Using the blackboard, have a coded message or a bit of information placed conspicuously for the kids to see as they arrive. Have your name in code for the kids to decipher. Also place the key on the board.

Codes are numerous: Morris Code, Braille, and numbers substituted for letters are common. Here is one that I use, formally called the Rosicrucian Cipher and based on a tic-tac-toe diagram.

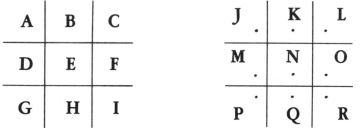

A	B	C
D	E	F
G	H	I

J .	K .	L .
M .	N .	O .
. P	. Q	. R

S ..	T ..	U ..
V ..	W ..	X ..
.. Y	.. Z	

The letter A is ⌐ , J is ⌐· , and S is ⌐·· ; while N is ·□ ; X is ·· ; and H is ⊓ .

Not only can the students decode any information or question that you put on the board, but they can send messages or create their own code. This simple introduction can be extended into a lengthier involvement.

Notes on this section . . . .

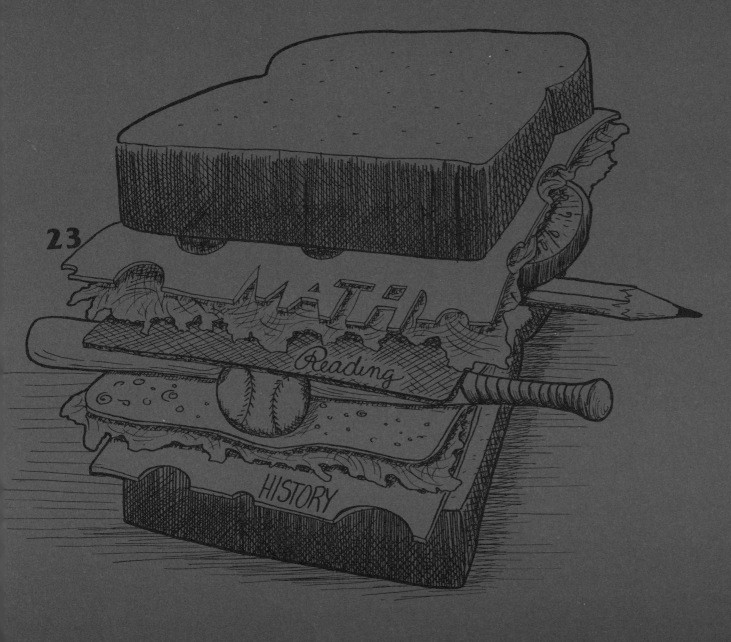

23

Introductions serve to bring a Substitute Teacher and the class closer together at the start of the morning. *Fillers* are quick inserts which carry this concept on, through remaining moments in the day. Fillers can be used as skillful transitions from one subject area to another; for example: an appropriate transition ending a math lesson or assignment and the introduction of a language arts presentation.

Fillers are also excellent attention directors after a recess or a period when physical activity has the kids wound up. Short, highly absorbing bits, Fillers serve to bring the students back to a composure necessary for subject matter presentations.

Then, there are always those few minutes of lag before it is your time to go to P.E. or your turn to go to lunch. Fillers will tide you over.

Kids are always judging you, the better you are able to interact with them the more comfortable will be your classroom stay. Fillers help to build this comfort and rapport so necessary for a positive classroom situation.

Here is a variety of Fillers — you may find some suitable for use as Introductions.

Stories

A selection of dependable short stories is a must for Substitute Teachers. Select stories that have a high absorption capability. Stories which accent novelty are especially good: quick, solvable mysteries;

abnormalities like Big Foot, the Abominable Snowman, the Loch Ness Monster, or supernatural encounters.

When I say short stories, I mean short, two to three minute readings. Short stories can also provide a lead-in to a creative writing assignment.

Initials

By using one or two letters from the alphabet, can you answer these?

an insect that stings	_____
a large body of water	_____
a question asked	_____
what the Fonz says	_____
a female sheep	_____
opposite of full	_____ _____
number after 79	_____ _____
a crawling plant	_____ _____
having many seeds	_____ _____
a tent	_____ _____
rot away	_____ _____

Did you answer **B, C, Y, A, U, MT, AT, IV, CD, TP, DK?**

Try these:

a green vegetable	_____
a blue bird	_____
a drink	_____
myself	_____
Spanish for yes	_____
pretty person	_____ _____
girl's name	_____ _____
boy's name	_____ _____
all right	_____ _____
jealousy	_____ _____
pajama	_____ _____
not difficult	_____ _____
a written composition	_____ _____

Use the blackboard or present orally. I like the kids to make-up several and to hand them in — from which I constantly enlarge my collection.

The way a baby would say the name of a chocolate cookie ___ ___ ___ (O E O)

Humor

Humor is not only a vehicle to build Substitute Teacher-student rapport, but if properly used it is a major influence upon learning. It can be used to accent positive behavior, to reveal a variety of human attitudes and values, and to affirm the simple joys of beauty and happiness. But most important, it is a subtle influence which can allow children to experience themselves in a relaxed, non-threatening context. If you have a conscious desire to affect learning (and not just cognitive learning), humor should be considered a significant influence toward that goal.

For Filler situations, humor can be used variously for relief, comment, example, or for pure enjoyment (sometimes I think enjoyment, because it is not an explicit district or state objective, is a forgotten classroom experience).

Joke telling is one format for humor. I rely on kids to give me joke material. I tell kids that I am willing to listen to jokes which are clean and which are not mean toward anyone. I go to the extent of writing jokes down that are new to me. When I make this effort, I enlist the kids to help me collect joke material, they are doing something for me (I use new material on my friends).

Jokes that kids present have certain characteristics of which you must be aware and with which you must deal in a fashion you determine appropriate. Students through the fifth-grade allow bodily functions to scintillate their jokes. For the post-fifth-graders, sexual awareness becomes — often blatantly — apparent. You will need to be able to handle such content.

Another facet which characterizes joke humor attaches oddity to a main character. Most often the main character is a less than mentally acute person or member of the specified ethnic culture. You will need to resolve how the butt character is stated.

I have a particular liking for visual humor which involves a student or the whole class. Such a liking recognizes the entertainment potential of the substitute teaching role. I especially like material such as the following *magic* trick.

A volunteer is selected and an exchange begins which includes both the volunteer and the class. To the volunteer:

"I am possibly one of the greatest, undiscovered magicians of our time. I have practiced many years to perfect my magic. You . . . are in luck. For right here, this very day and moment, I am going to

make a rabbit appear on your head. To accomplish this astounding feat, I will need your help. All you will need to do is to close your eyes, count to three, and open them slowly."

All banter — with appropriate gestures, exhortations, and facial contortions — to the volunteer and to the audience is to assure them that this is the most amazing feat they will ever see (build expectations).

Finally the volunteer must close her or his eyes and count. Once the eyes are opened: "Whether you believe it or not, there is now a rabbit on your head." Appeal to the class: "Isn't there!" Get them to respond by prompting a corral "yes."

The success of routines like this one depends on hamming-it-up, getting the kids excited, getting them with you, and then presenting the punch line.

Humor has its bounds — in addition to content. You certainly do not want the kids to desolve into a bunch of sillies for the rest of the day so that other work is obstructed. But moments of relief are fine chances to relate to kids. I even go so far as to tell the kids to take this *magic trick* home and perform it on a parent, a brother or sister, or even to perform it on the absent teacher when (s)he returns.

Humor has enormous teaching potential. I hope you will realize its teaching value — and its life value.

Math Square

Fillers can involve the entire class or they can be directed solely at individuals. For students who have nothing to do, or who have caught up on assignments, or who have finished early with an assignment, here is an activity.

This large square is composed of sixteen smaller squares. The sixteen squares — for this illustration — reinforce multiplication skills. The large square is composed by properly assembling the sixteen smaller squares.

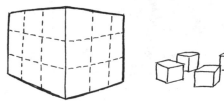

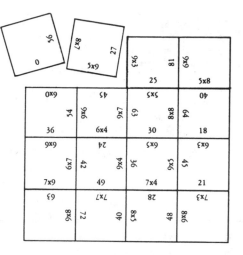

Before providing the activity to a student, you must have cut the large square — which has been designed for the appropriate operation — into its sixteen separate pieces and have placed those pieces into an envelope. The envelope is then given to the student.

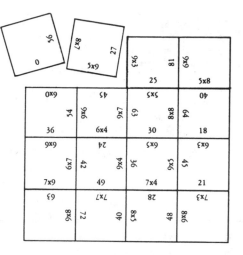

26

Students given the large square-form without any numbers can make their own squares for exchange — a lesson in itself.

63 · 9x8 · 7x9 · 72	9x9 · 6x7 · 36 · 42	0x9 · 54 · 9x6 · 45	0 · 56 · 8x7 · 27
7x7 · 40 · 49 · 9x4	24 · 6x4 · 9x7 · 45	5x9 · 8x5 · 36 · 63	9x3 · 28 · 7x4 · 48
6x9 · 9x5 · 30 · 8x8	5x5 · 25 · 81 · 8x6	45 · 7x3 · 21 · 64	9x9 · 6x9 · 18 · 40
5x9 · 8x6 · 7x7 · 9x8	72 · 40 · 8x5 · 48	28 · 8x6 · ...	7x3 · 8x8

Quicky Handouts

Handouts, sheets or half-sheets of paper that have a prepared activity are effective to gain immediate student attention and participation. Again, used as a change of pace or as a relief, handouts can draw upon various activities. Mazes find unanimous appeal with kids. The commercial market is full of maze styles (graph paper is an excellent resource allowing kids to create their own mazes. If done in heavy pencil, student created mazes can be reproduced by thermal heat and returned to the full class for solution).

Hidden pictures are another good source of quick handouts. Within a large overall picture is hidden a number of smaller objects. The kids must locate the hidden objects.

Be constantly on the lookout for unusual designs or novelties. They can be used for instant student absorption. For example, here is a design that spells the three letter word **FLY**.

Or, can you find an old woman and a young woman in this picture?

27

Hidden within this picture (right) are a number of animals. Can you find a monkey, a zebra, a giraffe, a leopard, a tiger, an elephant, and a bear?

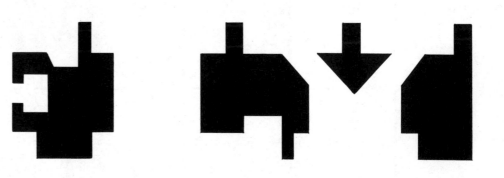

After Effect

Here is an "Ooooo, I can't believe my eyes," Filler. You will need several pieces of solid colored paper — construction paper does fine — and a bright back drop — a movie screen is excellent, or a light colored wall. Standing before the screen holding a piece of the colored paper, you might say:

"I'm going to hold this paper up against the screen for about a minute and a half. And when I take the paper away, keep your eyes focused on where the construction paper was. You should see something very interesting.

"Ready? Remember, I'm going to hold the paper up for you to stare at. If you don't want to participate, fine, don't bother the rest of us. Here goes."

Hold the paper against the bright back drop. You need to keep an encouraging and repetitious chatter going. A minute and a half is a long time.

When you drop your hand, be prepared for "oooo's" and "ahhhh's."

Although you may have held up a red piece of paper, when you drop your hand, another color will appear to the kids.

You can try other colors to see what colors, in turn, they produce. You can do several in succession, or you can spread them throughout the day.

The kids enjoy this. Besides the minute to a minute and a half time periods are probably the quietest and most composed minutes you will spend all day.

29

Newspaper Headlines

I need to take a brief opportunity to relate a story which I consider odd. Reading the newspaper, I came across a story that concerned a public official who hired a hit-man. It seems this official wanted to have done with an obstinate rival.

The hit-man was such a wacko that when he heard the convincing reasons stated by the official he agreed to do the job for a mere dollar. The hit-man, an Arty Something-or-other, went about the task.

Arty carried out the contract, strangling the politician's rival. Unfortunately, as Arty was leaving the scene of the crime, two people observed him. It was plain to them what Arty had done. Arty, consequently, had to strangle them, too.

The whole involved story came to light through the investigations of a dedicated newspaper reporter. The story's disclosure caused a sizeable scandal. The reporter's newspaper ran the exclusive with the headline, "Arty Chokes Three for a Dollar."

. . . . Sorry, could not resist that one.

Headlines, because they must be brief, often distort our language. How about these:

- Colt Born To Rancher With Two Heads
- Portland Rabbi Gives Birth To 14 Kittens
- Man Says He Left Large Ring In Hotel Bathtub
- Dealers Will Hear Car Talk At Meeting
- County Official To Talk Rubbish
- Grandmother Of 6 Makes Hole In One
- Lawyers Offer Poor Free Advice

Such headlines can be discussed for intended meanings. They are also lead-ins for students to write their own ambiguous headlines. I usually assign creation of at least one headline per student, to be handed in by a specified time. Depending upon how attentive the kids are and how the concept is presented, the results are usually quite good.

Antiquated Laws

Many states and cities have antiquated laws still in their judicial codes. These odd laws are often very amusing and spark the interest of kids.

- Men in Pine Island, Minnesota, must remove their hats when meeting a cow.
- A Florida law requires a person to keep his/her clothes on while bathing, even in his/her own home.
- In Berea, Ohio, animals out after dark must wear tail lights.
- You can not blindfold a cow on a public road in Arkansas.
- You can not tie a crocodile to a fire hydrant in Michigan.
- Tickling girls is illegal in Norton, Virginia.
- It is against the law to blow your nose in public in Waterville, Maine.
- Elephants can not drink beer in Natchez, Mississippi.
- In Seattle, Washington, it is against the law for a goldfish to ride a bus unless it lies still.
- It is against the law in California to set a mousetrap unless you have a hunting license.
- In Gary, Indiana, it is against the law to take a streetcar or go to a theater within four hours after eating garlic.

31

Life's Necessities

Here is a Filler that stimulates student thought, and allows the Substitute Teacher to entertain, too. It requires three simple props: a bag in which there is a small container of water and a small container of earth.

"In this bag are four things that life as we know it requires. I'm willing to listen to the ideas of anyone who raises a hand. What four elements are necessary for life to begin?"

Entertain guesses. Be prepared for strange guesses! Your ability to ham-it-up comes in handy for oddities.

When a student gets one of the four, affirm the correct answer by either bringing the element out of the bag or saying — as you secretively peer into the bag, "Yes, that's one of them."

You have two of the four components in containers, earth and water. The other two components can not be containerized — light and air. When light or air is given, you might peer into the bag and say, "Yes . . . (pause) light (or air) is in the bag. What else?"

Pun Names

I pay close attention to names. I find that they suggest certain qualities of character. Some names are melodious and some comic.

There once was a local band calling itself *Iguana Outside*. Think about that name as the slurred phrase . . . *you-go-on-outside*.

Could there be a law firm of *Holdum and Fleesum*? Or a person named *Norman Huble Bean*? Normal human being.

Beef Bullion suggests a thug to me, who might have a cowardly brother named *Chicken*.

The above pun names are a little sophisticated for most students, but pun names like the following are comprehensible:

U.R. Mean	Aunt Eater	Sandy Eggo
L.E. Phant	Polly Wog	Perry Chute
Bob Cat	Nita Bath	M.T. Skull
Ms. Fortune	Ali Gator	Downa Darkalley

Like joke Fillers, I (you may find another approach) enlist the kids' help to gather pun names. I set aside a blackboard space upon which they can add their pun names. As long as a name is not crude or a personal assault, and as long as they are not distractive to the class by walking to the board, students can write any and all creations.

I take time now and then to direct attention to new additions to the board and to provide other names I may know.

The Blackboard

The blackboard holds a strange appeal to most kids. I would guess it is so often a formal area that it takes on an aura of some magnitude. *Pun Names* serves to demystify the blackboard. Another and an imaginative use of the board involves fantasy.

Assign a segment of blackboard space as a special class area. At some height, draw a horizontal line across the area. The line represents the ocean, everything below is under water. Provide chalk (colored chalk is something even more special and alluring) and explain that the kids can draw, under certain circumstances (make rules), anything they want as long as it corresponds to an ocean theme.

Any restriction that you place on who might draw or when people might draw should be clearly stated and should be compatible with your lessons.

Besides underwater scenes, themes can be of outer space, the forest, city life, an airport, or a circus.

Coin You Believe It?

Did you hear about the magician who walked down the street and turned into a store? . . . Good, I did not want to walk through that one with you anyway. For the next bit of entertainment, you will need a penny, a dime, a volunteer, and a convincing patter like the *rabbit trick*.

Build up your astounding magical ability and to the volunteer say:

"Place the penny in one hand and the dime in the other. Don't let me see, but let everyone in class

An Unannounced Test

know in which hands the coins have been placed. I'll turn my back.

"To yourself, multiply what is in your right hand by 4 (or 6 or 8, any of the three will work). Don't tell me, but remember the product.

"Multiply what is in your left hand by 3 (or 5 or 7, any of the three will work).

"Add the two answers together. Tell us the total." (Wait for the total)

If the total is even, the penny is in the right hand. If the total is odd, the penny is in the left hand.

Gear the multiplication to the grade level. You might even use the blackboard to assist multiplying and adding by writing down, for example, in the patter above, what 3 times 1 is, or what 3 times 10 is. Or, since the class knows in which hands the coins are placed, they can be doing the operations, too. They, then, become a check for the volunteer's calculations.

Do you understand how this trick works? Something to do with place value.

With little or no explanation, hand out a sheet that has questions like the following:

Following Directions

Read all sentences carefully before doing anything on this page.

1. Write your name in the upper right hand corner of this page.
2. Write the date under your name.
3. On the back of this page, write:
   a. your address
   b. your phone number
   c. the names of your parents
   d. the name(s) of any brothers or sisters
   e. the name of any pet you have
4. Make three small circles in the upper left hand corner.
5. Put an 'X' in each circle.
6. Make three small holes with your pencil at the top of this page.
7. On the back of this page, add 707 and 123.
8. Put a circle around your name, then put a square around the circle.
9. Underline all even questions on this page.
10. If you have followed directions well, get up and tip-toe once around the room.
11. Count in a normal speaking voice from 1 to 10.
12. If you are the first person to get this far, call out, "I'm the first person to get this far, and I am a leader in following directions."
13. Tap your pencil on the desk 10 times.
14. Write 1 thru 10 at the bottom of this sheet.
15. Circle all 2's, 8's, and 9's on this sheet.
16. Now that you have read all of the directions, **do only** questions 1 and 2.

The Question Is . . . .

We are accustomed to being provided a question before we provide an answer. Turn the tables, provide the kids with answers to which they must pose questions.

Here are some answers:

Chip off the old block
Holy, moly schazam!
The Halls of Montezuma
We have to stop meeting
    like this

Go west young person
Ignore it and it will go
    away
A bird in the hand
    gathers no moss

I do not find the importance of this Filler to be in the novelty of the child's question as much as I feel its importance is in dealing with a situation in a different sequential context.

What floors take the most wax? (The Halls of Montezuma)

What do you call a piece of an old rock? (Chip off the old block)

More Stumpers

Not only are Stumpers excellent for Introductions, but they serve equally as well for Fillers. Here is a wide variety which calls for greater involvement than the Stumpers already presented.

An archer must make a score of 74. What combinations must be aimed for?

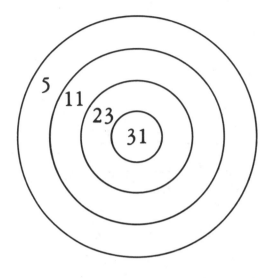

If the archer must score 100 on this target, what combinations must be aimed for?

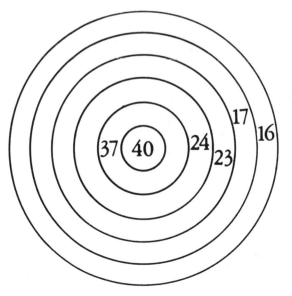

Erase 6 of 9 digits in the following numbers so that the 3 remaining digits add up to 20.

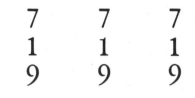

Erase 9 of 15 digits to add up to 1,111.

1 1 1
3 3 3
5 5 5
7 7 7
9 9 9

Put the digits 1, 2, 3, 4, 5 in the circles so that the sum of 3 numbers in each direction is the same. Find as many different ways as you can.

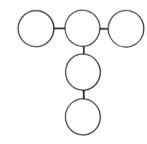

Draw a figure like the one shown here. Put the digits 2, 3, 4, 5, 6, 7, 8 in the circles so that the sum of any line is equal to 15.

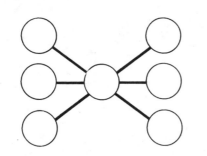

Place a sentence, paragraph, or passage on the board from which vowels have been removed.

Y cn rd wtht vwls f y wrk hrd. Smtms t's sy, smtms t's hrd!

Remove letter parts (ascenders, descenders, legs, etc.).

⌐hc ooo ˙s wooo˙no h˙s to˙l

(The dog is wagging his tail)

Change one letter at a time, make at least six different words. bean —

bean
lean
lead
leer
deer
dear
bear
boar

Other words: try, sack, rock, most, gold.

Make as many sentences as possible using the following skeletal form:

S_____ ____ _____f _____

(Swimming is always fun)

B___ m_____ a_____ n_____

Tongue Twisters.

Tongue twisters always delight. They also provide good practice for a handwriting exercise.

- Francis Fletcher fried fifty flounders for Fatty Fifer's father.
- Old oily Ollie oils old oily autos.
- Six slippery sliding snakes slither swiftly.
- The clothes moth's mouth closed.
- A skunk sat on a stump. The stump said the skunk stunk. The skunk said the stump stunk. Who stunk? The skunk or the stump?

Match Sticks.

- Equations
  Move 1 match and make this equation true.

Remove 2 matches and make this equation true.

Move 1 match and make this equation true.

Move 1 match and make this equation true.

Move 2 matches and make this equation true.

35

■ Squares

Remove 3 matches and leave 3 squares.

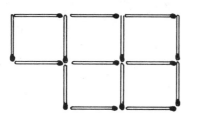

Remove 5 matches, leaving 3 squares all the same size.

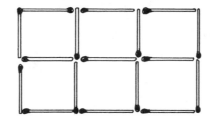

■ Other shapes

Remove 4 matches and leave 4 triangles.

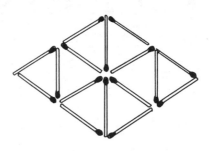

Remove 4 matches and leave 5 squares.
Remove 6 matches and leave 5 squares.

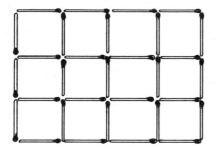

Remove 2 matches, leaving 2 squares (they may not be the same size).

Remove 4 matches and leave 9 squares.

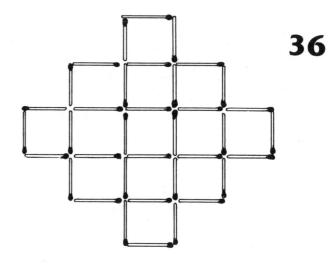

Move 2 matches to make 4 squares.

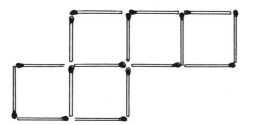

Remove 6 matches, leaving 2 squares (they may be of equal size).

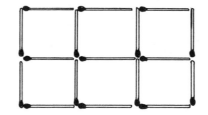

Notes on this section . . . .

39

Introductions and Fillers are short, quickly paced presentations. They serve to build rapport, to relieve tedium, to spark interest, and to redirect student thought. In combination with lengthier *Subject Area* presentations, they provide a full and meaningful school day.

Subject Area presentations require considered thought. Around what should they be composed? The reinforcement of basic skills? The simple enjoyment of something new and different? I feel that reinforcement of basic skills and enjoyment in something new are significant offerings. Skills can always use reinforcement. And enjoyment as an experience in personal development is a subtle student benefit gained from a Substitute Teacher's planning.

Lesson planning by regular classroom teachers is predominantly segmented. There may be plans for reading, math, science, and art, all as independent disciplines and seemingly unrelated. Some planning is very structured owning to the teacher or to the composure of the kids. Other planning is looser, with students assuming a varying responsibility for their work.

I would like to present for this Subject Area section a small variety of Subject Area lessons. While the lessons cover different curriculum areas, they are not organized into appropriate groups such as science lessons, math lessons, or language arts lessons. Other commercial materials for Substitute Teachers deal heavily with lessons thus categorized. You might further benefit from consulting them

not only for their content, but for their teaching style as well (see Bibliography).

Subject Area lessons should be planned with attention on the length of time a Substitute Teacher can expect to remain in an assignment. Since most assignments are a day or two in length, a large number of Subject Area lessons should be planned for this type of stay. These lessons will require quick presentations and results. But for those assignments which last for several days, Subject Area planning can allow for lengthier teacher preparation and lengthier student involvement. Whatever the length of assignment, a Substitute Teacher must not only prepare solid lessons, but gather and assemble the materials that will support the preparation and presentation.

The following lessons must be viewed as adaptable, not only for grade level, but for your style of teaching and the period of time available for their presentation.

40

Fill-in Completions

41

Fill-ins can be presented as an oral or a written activity. I prefer them as a written activity. Students are provided a story — the more humorous the better — from which certain key words are missing — certain nouns, verbs, adjectives, exclamations, etc. Students rewrite the story inserting the appropriate words. The kids can be as crazy or as serious as they want. Sharing the results of the activity is always an enjoyable part of the lesson.

You need not purchase materials, you can take an appropriate paragraph or page and, say, omit every fifth word. Or students can create Fill-in scripts for you.

Other variations of Fill-in ideas can be used for verse, songs, or recipes. Songs, like *Oh, Susana*, are excellent for the younger grades, simply omit key words.

The Fill-in idea can be extended from substituting just one word to creating whole new phrases — prepositional phrases, adjective-noun combinations, adverb-verb combinations, entire noun phrases, certain clauses, etc. Developing this exercise — especially good for poetry — requires your being very clear as to what type of words or word groupings are to be changed.

Still another variation of this Fill-in lesson is the pass-on story. Here is the skeletal form for a pass-on story:

Line - 1. Student's own name
     2. and _____
     3. went _____
     4. to get a_____
     5. and they saw _____.
     6. They ate _____
     7. and _____ said, "_____,"
     8. so they_____.

Have the students fold a piece of paper into eight sections (demonstrate) and number each section, 1 to 8. The students put their name in box 1 and fold that box back.

I explain that they will be getting their own paper back, but for the second step they must exchange their paper with someone. I give them a quick five seconds and then continue:

"In the second box, the box with the *2* in it, write the word *and*. Remember the first sentence has your name, now for box 2 you need another name — someone you know, or a famous person maybe. Fill-in box 2. (pause) You have five seconds to exchange . . . .

(after five seconds) "In box 3, write *went to* and then a place someone might go — home, the moon, crazy, whatever you want. (pause)

Ready. . . . . . ."

Continue for all eight lines, the eighth person will return the completed story to the person listed in box 1. The kids enjoy reading the creations aloud.

Fill-in completions have a wide variety of possibilities, kids enjoy them.

Did You Hear?

I find particular accent for lessons which get kids to participate actively in an exercise, something beyond the seatwork that is done on a solitary basis. Different classes have different ability levels when it comes to active participation. Some classes handle active participation well, others find participation a chance for rowdiness.

Did You Hear is a formula adventure. It requires kids, on their own or in combination, to fashion a story that seesaws back and forth between peril and safety, usually resolving itself humorously. Sharing creations is a big part of the lesson.

Here are three examples that can serve to prepare the students for their own creations. These examples are student creations. Following the three examples is the skeletal form of the adventure.

Ann: Did you hear about Mark T?.
Nan: No, what happened?
Ann: He fell from a tall building.
Nan: Aw, that's too bad.
Ann: But he caught hold of a pole.
Nan: Hey, that's good.
Ann: But it broke.
Nan: Aw, that's too bad.
Ann: But he climbed into a window before it broke.
Nan: Hey, that's good.
Ann: But a lady threw him out again.
Nan: Aw, that's too bad.
Ann: But there were firemen to catch him.
Nan: Hey, that's good.
Ann: But they weren't watching.

Ann: Did you hear about Sally?
Nan: No, what happened.
Ann: She fell out of a tree.
Nan: Aw, that's too bad.
Ann: But there was a trampoline below.
Nan: Hey, that's good.
Ann: But it had a hole in it.
Nan: Aw, that's too bad.
Ann: But she missed the hole.
Nan: Hey, that's good.
Ann: But she started to bounce on the trampoline.
Nan: Aw, that's too bad.
Ann: But she bounced back into the tree.
Nan: Hey, that's good.
Ann: But she fell and broke her leg.

Ann: Did you hear about poor John?
Nan: No, what happened?
Ann: He fell out of a helicopter.
Nan: Aw, that's too bad.
Ann: But he had an umbrella.
Nan: Hey, that's good.
Ann: But it broke.
Nan: Aw, that's too bad.
Ann: But there was a big lake below.
Nan: Hey, that's good.
Ann: But there was a shark in the lake.
Nan: Aw, that's too bad.
Ann: But he missed the shark.
Nan: Hey, that's good.
Ann: But he missed the lake too.

Ann: Did you hear about _____?
Nan: No, what happened?
Ann: He/she_____.
Nan: Aw, that's too bad.
Ann: But he/she _____.
Nan: Hey, that's good.
Ann: But _____.
Nan: Aw, that's too bad.
Ann: But _____.
Nan: Hey, that's good.
Ann: But _____.
Nan: Hey, that's too bad.
Ann: But he/she_____.
Nan: Hey, that's good.
Ann: But he/she_____.

Beat the Teacher

Beat the Teacher is an excellent lesson to reinforce a desired computational skill. Students are given an answer sheet (which you will have to make) prepared for the operation to be tested. For our purpose here, let us use multiplication. The answer sheet would have a series of spaces like:

_____ × _____ = _____ _____

_____ × _____ = _____ _____

The teacher reads a problem and an answer. The student copies down the problem and the answer. If the answer to the problem is correct, the student does nothing more. If the problem is incorrect, the student must correct the problem. For instance, if the teacher says, "Six times eight equals forty-seven," the student writes in the space:

___6___ × ___8___ = ___47___ _____ .

Knowing that 6 x 8 ≠ 47, the student would (hopefully) correct the problem by crossing out 47 and next to it write 48.

___6___ × ___8___ = ~~47~~ ___48___

You might want to mix operations, in which case the answer sheet does not provide an operation and would look like:

_____ _____ = _____ _____

You need to prepare a list of facts and an answer sheet that will satisfy your expected teaching needs.

43

Name Pin-ons

You know the game *Twenty Questions*. Here is a variation that involves considerable student interaction. Pick a grouping (set) that has a large and a familiar number of members, for instance: vegetables, occupations, fruits, trees, states, cities. On small slips of paper write as many — for example — occupations as you can — about half again as many as you have students. These slips will be pinned to the back of each student. The student must determine by an agreed upon or stated method of questioning, what occupation is written on his or her slip.

Once a student has determined his or her pin-on, he or she comes up to you for another one.

You can allow the kids to mill about the room asking questions or you can have them divide into groups and proceed in an orderly fashion asking questions. I would suggest the latter. I usually ask the kids to divide into groups of five or six — I can assign the groups, or they can be voluntarily formed.

You must stress one thing. They are forbidden to tell another what that student's slip says. You can make a rule that questions can only be answered *yes* or *no*.

You should briefly put across the idea of asking questions which narrow possibilities. They should not be continually asking, "Am I this?", "Am I that?"

The activity lasts as long as the enthusiasm does.

Postcards

Designing a postcard provides an interesting and an involved format, combining creativity, art, and writing. Upon an index card of desired size or tagboard of desired size have students design a special postcard.

Students are to use both sides of the postcard; upon one side they can create a design or picture, and upon the other they can address their card and write comments or salutations. Some students will be so replete as to include unique stamps and postmarks.

Themes are endless: social studies units, vacations, scenes from books, jokes, movies. Written comment can emphasize handwriting and vary in tone from humorous to serious.

You might consider shopping for or collecting postcards prior to student participation. Cards obtained in such a fashion can provide incentive and example for the student creations.

Good News, Bad News

Your luxurious 737 is cruising along when the voice of the stewardess comes over the address system:

"Ladies and gentlemen, I have some good news and some bad news to report.

"The bad news is that our sophisticated navigational equipment has totally failed and we have no idea of our present location.

"Now, for the good news: we are ahead of schedule."

The *Good News-Bad News* routine has become a comedy classic. Kids find it an enjoyable exercise. Although the routine is short, it requires a great deal of the kids. The creative process of a comic delivery requires significant internalization.

A routine can be presented very simply, as:

Good news, Mom, I finally bought some snowshoes. Bad news, they were sandals.

Mrs. Randall, I have some good news. Your husband won the tree climbing contest, but I have some bad news too. A bear was chasing him.

Bad news: Your Honda just drove off the rim of the Grand Canyon.
Good news: It got 54 miles to a gallon on the way down.
Or Good News-Bad News routines can be elaborately cast in character, verbage, and setting:

The hired hand came in, "Mrs. Brown, I've got some good news and some bad. First the good. You know that cow you couldn't get to give milk? Well, I got it to. Now the bad. She gives blackberry flavored milk."

Slavemaster to the slaves below deck: "Good news men! At the next port there will be food and grog for everyone. Bad news: the captain wants to go water skiing this afternoon."

An African dictator: "My beloved citizens, today I stand before you to report some good news and some bad news. First the bad news. The crops have failed and we have nothing left to eat but lizards. Now for the good news, there aren't enough lizards to go around."

The principal called Mr. and Mrs. Wombat and said: "I have some good news about your son, Igor. For the first time since he began attending our school, Igor took a shower in gym class. Unfortunately, he forgot to take off his clothes."

Creating Good News-Bad News routines is fairly spontaneous. Encourage kids to read their creations. While some are reading theirs aloud, others can be writing. Most kids will write several routines. Also encourage kids to elaborate on characters and setting.

Here is a *clothing* one that may be gross, but one that kids (myself being one — how does he mean that?) enjoy:

An Army Drill Instructor talking to his recruits (the DI has to have a Brooklyn accent): "All right men. Good news. Today you get a change of underwear. Bad news: Wolowski you change with Farinetti, Farinetti you change with Cohn, Cohn you change with Mitsoboshi . . . ."

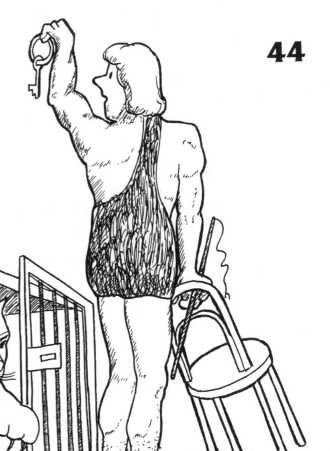

Book Covers

Making book covers, that will go to cover a specific book, prove an interesting activity. You must locate paper large enough to cover an average book. Butcher paper that comes from rolls or large sheets of art paper are good sources for book covers.

Kids must first be shown how to fit the paper to their book — math book, science book, library book. Once the form is obtained, the students can create their special cover. They can illustrate the cover and add lettering to complete their creations. Covers can be for fictitious books, or a scene from a cherished book, a social science unit, movie scenes, designs. The inside slip-cover can even contain writing, giving a review or a synopsis of the book.

The Facts Matrix

Facts Matrix, like Beat the Teacher, reinforces specific mathematical operations — addition, subtraction, multiplication, or division. Below is a multiplication matrix.

Kids must determine what factors when placed in the boxes of the top row and the side row will provide the appropriate product within the components of the larger square. Sporatic answers are provided within the larger square that will lend clues to factor patterns.

Part of the lesson helps kids understand how to determine factors and products appropriate for the specific boxes. The other part of the lesson is to get kids to create their own matrix. Student created matrices can be reproduced by thermal heat process for distribution the next day. Or students can exchange their matrices with each other for immediate solution.

Your directions to get students started on matrix construction need to stress several points: (1.) how big is the large square to be? 10 by 10? 12 by 12?; and (2.) there must be sufficient clue-answers within the large square to assist solution — I would suggest that a rule be made that each row, vertical and horizontal within the large square, must contain at least two clue-answers.

For an excellent perspective of what the kids will encounter, sit down and complete the matrix below.

X	1			7				4
9				63				
		6			12			
5		50	40					
				70		90		
		40					20	
3			24					12
7					14	35		
8						72		32

Nonsense Stories

Kids have a certain fascination for nonsense words. The sound combinations that they can construct prove endless. Here is a simple lesson that uses nonsense words in a brief story.

I usually ask them to listen to some short stories I have written using nonsense words:

Hi, I'm your everyday Substitute **Gleep**! I go to **clarn** everyday and teach weird **ruds** how to be sweet little **tookies** and nice, all around **grossers**. Sometimes I get very **narnish**. I stamp my **stabes**, wave my **vankies**, and shout at the top of my **gibbles**.

One day while walking my **lum**, I tripped over a huge **stabe**. I fell and almost broke my **feeks**. Boy, what a narrow escape. Luckily I landed on my **vank**. Later that day I had a **harning** laugh over the mishap.

One dark and **cleep** morning, I arrived at _____ School. All these weird **ruds** were running around in Ms./Mr. _____'s class. I grabbed a large **tharp** and hit one of the wild **ruds** over the **mant**. It fell to the floor kicking and screaming. Somebody gave it a glass of **hibe** and it recovered.

Holy **clarn**! Look at all those **zops**. Why they are so **haring** that no one would want to have one for a pet. They probably eat **vank** tons a day and howl at the **mogs** at night.

I list a number of nonsense words on the board. I include words that have various endings. Such variations (ed, ing, es, y) will encourage certain word functions — verbs, nouns, adjectives, etc.

Here are further examples, this time from elementary school students:

One **breet vank** night, I heard a **tharp manting** at the **dant**. It was very **clarn**. I went out and saw a **lum filch**. I ran away. I ran into a **ribe** with some **feeks**. A **tharp** jumped out of the bushes and tried to **stabe** me. It was afraid of **ruds**, so I showed it a **rud** and it ran away and I went home.

One night I was playing **harning** and along came a **tharp**. He bit my **cleep** and then I fell into a **mant**. But soon a **hipe** came along and threw me a **rud**. Then I climbed out and went to **lum**.

Encourage kids to write several stories, making the stories as strange, or as silly, or as far out, or as serious as you or they desire. Encourage creation of their own nonsense words. Have select students read their creations. Keep the process of creating stories and reading products going simultaneously.

46

Shirt Designs

Personalized shirts have become quite popular. Names, slogans, figures, or pictures are easily transferred onto shirts to satisfy a purchaser's desire. Kids are especially attracted to personalized clothing, particularly when it comes to fantastic scenes and descript sayings.

Shirt designing can become an elaborate project for kids. First, they will need to design a shirt in small scale. Provide them with a shirt-form — on, say, 8½ by 11 paper — that will serve as a planning model. Second, larger sheets of paper will serve to bring their small scale creations to actual size.

If paper is abundant, a shirt front and back can be designed and decorated. Front and back, once completed, can be stapled together and the creation donned. If this is the case, a fit-all shirt pattern made of sturdy cardboard is a must.

47

Stations

Choose a subject area. Assemble four or five packets, the contents of which reinforce specific skills within that subject matter area.

Each packet should contain an activity that will occupy four to six students for ten to fifteen minutes. The packet should be self-explanatory — although you can give instructions, too — and contain simple materials that require student participation. Maybe you will require something to be handed in to verify student participation. Or, maybe just the experience of taking part in the activity is enough.

Place the packets about the room and indicate that each is a *Station*. The students will rotate from Station to Station performing the packet activity. With five packets, five students to a packet, for ten minutes, this activity can occupy twenty-five students for fifty minutes. It is best to have students remain in the same five-person group as that group moves from Station to Station.

Stations is a lesson concept that works best with a class that responds well to its Substitute Teacher and that responds well to the movement and interaction necessary to participate in each Station. The planning and assembling of each Station is also important to the success of this lesson.

Longer Activities

Most substitute teaching assignments last for a day or two at the most. Lessons which can be presented and results gained within short time spans prove the best for these typical assignments. But if you are in an assignment for a lengthier period, lessons which allow for more time and involvement are necessary.

Word Searches

Word Searches are plentiful. Countless pulps are published monthly specializing in Word Searches. Kids seem to enjoy them. Yet I often fail to recognize the educational value of just giving kids Word Search after Word Search, even if the search reinforces a special topic. After a point saturation brings disinterest.

Word Searches can become a lesson which only partially involves solving a specific, topical search. I have a short story from my experience:

Once upon a time several kids saw that I was trying to compose a Word Search. They wanted to try it too, so to be rid of them while I did my work, I gave each a piece of quarter-inch graph paper. They took it upon themselves to construct a Word Search on a subject of their own choosing. One chose the presidents of the United States; one chose major rivers of the United States; one decided to write everyone's last name into a search; others chose subjects that varied from animals to cars. The most important feature of the whole

situation was that they took it upon themselves to use resource materials to find out about their respective topics.

Certainly they did not learn everything about their topics in the process of research, but they were sparked into using resource materials. And to my knowledge, they have been happily Word Searching ever after.

Getting kids involved in creating a Word Search is more important to me than padding their time with a Word Search on, say, exotic fish. Relevancy is a key to interest, getting kids going on what interests them. Not only allow kids to create a search on a topic of their choosing, but have them make a copy of their search which can be reproduced by thermal heat. Or give them a ditto master on which they can place their final work. Students take a certain added interest in solving their classmates' creations. You can be selective about which Word Searches will be reproduced; or you can have students work in pairs, thus reducing the number that would need reproduction.

One interest grabber that is effective either late in the first day of an assignment — if you find the time — or during the second day is to provide the kids with a Word Search that has incorporated their names — first, last, or both.

48

Front Page

This lesson requires you to gather an assortment of materials and it also requires that you take time to familiarize the kids with the contents of a newspaper. The results of the lesson are impressive.

Kids have a varied awareness of newspaper contents: it has different sections, it has pictures, it has a mast-head, it has a table to direct you for contents, etc. If you can, get a front page from several different papers, the contrasting layout and format will serve as good example.

I generally post several front pages about the room, drawing attention to similarities and contrasts.

Before kids launch into creating their own front pages, you will need to gather the following: a number of front pages, paper — preferably butcher type — which is as large or larger than an actual front page, and pictures — newspapers continually junk wire service photos; I have merely gone to my local paper and asked for them. If wire photos are not available, magazine pictures serve, or kids can draw their own.

Students — individually or in small groups — tape an actual front page to a large window. The butcher paper is then taped over the front page. Students trace the outline of the front page (not actual mast-head or article captions) to give appropriate areas for columns, articles, and pictures. From this skeleton, they can create (fill-in) material according to column space and add appropriate pictures.

They can draw from any section of the newspaper for front page news — sports, weather, obituaries, etc. Stories can be nonsensical, topical, local, as they desire.

You can act as city editor for consultation, article ideas, and proofing.

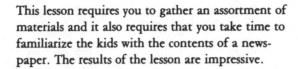

Comics

Ask the kids to bring a section from the Sunday Comics or an old comic book to class. Plan ahead in making this request and state it numerous times. The kids are to choose a comic strip panel for reproduction. Reproducing the one scene will involve measurement, scale, and proportion.

A grid, quarter-inch or five millimeter scale is best, is drawn on the original comic panel. A larger grid is drawn on a much larger sheet of drawing paper or butcher paper -two inch or five centimeter scale is good. By transferring what is within the smaller grid of the comic strip to the larger grid of the paper, the character and scene are enlarged.

Sounds simple enough, heh? You will be amazed to find how many kids do not know which of those marks on the ruler represents a quarter inch or five millimeters. You'll be amazed to find how many students can not draw a straight line using a straight edge, and many have absolutely no concept of proportion or scale.

Your presentation, should you accept it Mr./Ms. Substitute Teacher, will need to include pointed information on ruler measurements, gridding (and bearing it), and scale transfer from the original strip to the enlarged size. You will need to make sure there are adequate rulers, yardsticks and metersticks, rubber erasers, and materials to color or paint the enlarged scene.

This lesson is involved, fun, and very challenging (almost an obstacle) for students. Kids must solve significant problems to enlarge their comics.

The Road Map Game or Drivin' 'em Crazy

You are going to be a favorite at the local gas station, the local Chamber of Commerce, or at hotel-motels which provide complementary maps. All of your kids will need a map — state, national, or local. You can request and request the students to bring a map. But you had better be prepared and accumulate as many maps as you can.

Each student will need a map and fifteen (you can vary the number) cards or slips of paper. Students are to plan a round trip with fifteen check points. They can make side trips, use any highway or trail they want. The route and the check points must be outlined — accented in crayon or marking pen. Each check point has a question that can be answered from the use of the map — distance between nearby points, town populations, direc-

tions, symbols. Answers to the questions are written on the back of the appropriate cards or slips. Once the trip is planned and the questions written, the game is ready for use.

A student, or a group of students, plays the game by taking the route and stopping at each check point to answer the question. The maker of the game oversees its use and serves as final authority and question checker. The game can be played just to make the circuit or a time factor can be included for competition.

The whole process includes game making and game playing. The playing portion can extend on and on and on. . . . It's a real trip.

#12

And Now A Word From Our Sponsor...

I often wonder when some fringe artist who covers as a part-time college instructor and cannery worker will begin a chore to compile and catalogue, if not to obtain a federal grant to erect a repository for, commercial art — commercial art as in t.v., radio, and billboard advertisements. Our waking hours are so bombarded with sight and sound messages for soaps, preparations, appliances, machines, and beverages that someone is bound to identify a common element to all such messages and proclaim it a new art form.

Anyway, this lesson is a parody on advertisement. While it can include serious aspects of consumerism, it is directed at the creation of a fictitious product to be promoted.

Kids will need to bring a product container — a cereal box, a large can, a bag. They are to redecorate their container, creating a new product. The new product is to be as flashy and appealing as possible. It may include snappy slogans, a statement of contents, cooking or baking or mixing instructions, or a testimonial. You will need to make sure that materials are available for redecoration — paper, scissors, glue, paint, etc.

Creating the packaging is only part of the process. They — this can be an individual or a small group undertaking — can also create a presentation for their product. The presentation can be written down. Or product presentations can be given before the class, depending to what extent the kids are involved. Encourage slogans, jingles, scene portrayals, what have you.

Introducing the entire lesson is done well by holding a discussion on advertising. Get the kids involved in ads they like or dislike and what ads are selling.

You might gather containers to bring for those who forget theirs.

Guided Fantasies

I find that children have the most astounding imaginations. And I also find that the most significant glimpses of their imaginations too often come in other than teacher directed learning situations. Why is that?

Imagination is a quality that is easily downgraded or dismissed by adults. For it is, perhaps by explanation, not the type of activity or training that adults perceive as necessary for the realities of the everyday world. Despite such an explanation, I consider exercise of one's imagination an important skill. Fantasy journeying, as guided by a teacher, is an activity which allows great imaginative exercise.

A *Guided Fantasy* is an experience that each child has a unique opportunity to control. The guide-teacher sets a general format for the journey, suggesting key figures, activities, or occurrences, the details of which are left to each student to actively construct.

Kids participate in a journey by relaxing and closing their eyes. Helping the kids to relax and to get settled is important. A relaxation exercise used as a prelude to the actual journey is useful. Such an exercise can concentrate on the physical sensations of breathing, body warmth, blood flow, or musculature. Once settled and relaxed, a journey may go

53

This section illustrated by Phyllis Helland

like this:

You are becoming very small, shrinking down to about six inches . . . Walk around the room and investigate it from your new size . . . Walk over here to the door . . . We're going to leave the room (building, school) and take a walk outside on this trail (the trail is a control that always allows the kids to return to the classroom). Anytime you want to leave us, you can always walk back to the room . . . Let's start walking . . . Over there, just off the trail, is something that catches your eye . . . Take a long look at this interesting object . . . Let's move on . . . We're entering the woods now . . . And just ahead, through the trees we see a meadow . . . We stop at the edge of the meadow and look it over . . . The grass is soft and warmed by the sun . . . There are wildflowers of many colors and smells . . . We'll play in the meadow for a few moments . . . Look at that old tree on the other side of the meadow, the one with the large roots that go into the ground . . . There is a hole by the roots . . . Let's walk down into the hole and see what is under the tree . . . Follow me, leave room for the others. We'll be coming out this same way, too . . . Did you feel the change in tempera-

54

ture? . . . The last time I was here I saw some furry creatures . . . Keep walking . . . Look, over there . . . Quiet, don't scare them . . . It is time to leave, we'll go back the way we came . . . Now, we need to get back to the classroom quickly . . . As we walk into the meadow, with each step we get bigger . . . And bigger . . . And bigger, until we can walk over the trees . . . In a few steps we are back to school . . . As we walk across the playground, we shrink back to normal size . . . When you are ready, you may open your eyes.

I would like to recant my reaction to the first Guided Fantasy I ever presented to children. Upon conclusion of the fantasy, I asked the kids what they had experienced at various parts during the journey. The individual responses, and the eagerness of the kids to share their experiences, shocked me. The way the kids responded led me to think that they were not only putting me on, but they were, each and every one of them, conspiring to put me on. My reaction was partially the gross underestimation of the ability that children have to respond to voice suggestion, and partially the influence of my adult frame of reference which had long ago outgrown such childish activity.

I wanted to tell of my reaction to prepare you for the unexpected. Student responses are utterly amazing . . . unbelievable, if one is not prepared.

Psychotherapists have explored fantasy as a tool to devulge the inner world of a person and as a key to remedy thinking disorders. A Substitute Teacher has neither the time nor the license to conduct a fantasy journey with either of these intentions. But they can rightly, and simply, use directed fantasy to give practice to mental skills which stimulate imagination, imagery, listening, and creativity.

For the Substitute Teacher who will use fantasy journeying in his or her teaching, it can only be done well in a setting that includes the complete cooperation of the students. A Substitute Teacher will need to have established an excellent rapport with the kids. Maybe the Substitute Teacher will need to be in the class several days or on several different occasions before the proper cooperative atmosphere is conducive to the lesson.

Kids can tune in and out of the journey with remarkable speed. A student can turn from socking a friend to quick immersion in the guide's setting. Some kids will *get lost*, so to speak, during a journey only to create their own travels.

The fantasy journeying can be a spark for creative

writing assignments or art lessons. "What did you see beside the trail? Describe it in words and draw it."

Remember, you are not a practicing psychologist. Journeying is for fun and enjoyment, mental exercise, imaginative and creative exploration.

Here is another journey:

You are a traveler in a foreign country. You have just gotten off the train and stepped into a market place. Take a complete look around the market place . . . Listen to all the sounds . . . Walk around and explore . . . What do you see? . . . What one thing attracts your attention? . . . Move closer to it and find out more about it . . . What makes it so attractive? . . . Look at it closely from all angles . . . Touch it . . . Now move to the edge of the market place . . . Look far off . . . You'll see something in the distance moving toward you . . . As it comes nearer, you will be able to see it more clearly . . . It stops in front of you . . . Have a conversation with it . . . The train whistle just sounded. You've got to go . . . Say good-bye and make your way across the market place . . . Board the train and wave good-bye . . . When you're ready, open your eyes and return to the classroom.

MAGIC
CARPETS

58

Notes on this section . . . .

Selected Bibliography

The periodical writings on substitute teaching or the Substitute Teacher are not great. *Not great*, perhaps, is best understood in a dual sense, not many in number and poor, generally, in content for those published.

Teacher training institutions, educational researchers, school cirriculum administrators, classroom teachers, and Substitute Teachers themselves have failed to provide the substitute teaching role with the writing that is needed to help establish substitute teaching as an integral and a respectable part of daily education. Daily public education does not stop with the absence of a teacher, classes are not dismissed for the duration of a teacher's absence. If daily education is to continue and if Substitute Teachers are to carry on in the absence of a regular classroom teacher, greater attention must be provided the role of the Substitute Teacher. One means of attention is through writings which relate to the many facets of the substitute teaching role. At present, writings are not great. (End of tirade.)

This bibliography lists a number of periodical articles which best (in my subjective opinion) attempt to deal with substitute teaching. These articles are grouped into four sections: For the Substitute Teacher, For the Regular Classroom Teacher, For the Administrator, and Substitute Teaching. In some instances the same article will be listed in more than one section. Because an article is listed under a specific section, a teacher, for example, should not exclude reference to the other sections for further pertinent information. Many of the articles are briefly capsulized.

This bibliography also includes the major commercial books and pamphlets published expressly for Substitute Teachers. Prices and publishers accompany the products listed.

For the Substitute Teacher

Beaman, Sarah G. *For You or Your Substitute. . . 20 Ways to Keep Them Learning While You're Trying to Get Your Head Straight,* Teacher, October 1972, pages 59–61.
- 20 activities that "can be geared to any age or reading level."

Davis, Alonalie H. *Substitute Portfolio: 20 Ways to Make Your Day Easier,* Instructor, October 1975, pages 100–101.
- Techniques "to help your day proceed more smoothly."

Educational Resources Information Center (ERIC) ERIC Database. *Substitute Teachers: The Best of ERIC on Educational Management,* No. 79, February 1985, ED 253971, www.eric.org.
- Annotated bibliography reviewing 12 publications dealing with substitute teaching.

Freedman, Miriam K. *Strategies for Substitutes,* Teacher, October 1976, pages 68–75.
- 18 techniques to make lesson plans more effective.

Harwood, Shirley K. *Substitute Survival Kit,* Instructor, November 1970, pages 16–17.
- General ideas for a survival kit.

Lester, Michael C. *Survival Guide for Substitutes,* Saturday Review of Education, April 1973, pages 51–52.
- 8 ideas: math, social studies, English, any class. Aimed at upper elementary and middle school.

Lovley, Sharon. *A Practical Guide to Substituting at Different Grade Levels,* Teacher PreK–8, October 1994, pages 70–71.
- Suggestions and activities to use with different grade levels and to develop an appropriate teaching style.

62

Miller, Peggy. *To A Substitute: You Are A Professional Educator,* Instructor, August 1974, pages 134–136.
- "(S)pecific behaviors substitute teachers must act out in order to create new role expectations." 21 suggestions.

Pronin, Barbara. *Guerilla Guide to Effective Substitute Teaching,* Instructor, February 1983, pages 64–66.
- Suggestions how substitutes can introduce themselves, gain class respect, avoid discipline problems. Classroom games and activities listed.

Seldon, Marian. *Especially for Substitute Teachers,* Instructor, March 1972, pages 23–24.
- 13 ideas focusing on the primary grades: writing, reading, math, art, songs, indoor games.

Wolff, Diana. *Substitute Portfolio: Letting Behavior Mod Work for You,* Instructor, October 1975, pages 101–102.

Zjawin, Dorothy. *Shorts for Subs: 25 Activities for Short Notice Subbing,* Instructor, February 1978, pages 71–72.
- 21 ideas: math and reading.

For the Regular Classroom Teacher

Davis, Alonalie H. *20 Ways to Make Your Day Easier,* Instructor, October 1975, pages 100–101.
- Suggestions for teachers, et al, to make a substitute's day proceed smoothly.

Funk, Betty D. *Substitutes Need Your Help,* Instructor, November 1974, page 26.
- "(T)o maintain harmony, teachers should take time to discuss" their absences with their children. 6 principles.

Just What the Substitute Ordered, Learning,
August 1996, pages 75–76.
- Class meetings in preparation for substitute teachers.

Keller, Sara Ann. *Dear Teacher, While You Were Gone . . . ,* Teacher, October 1976, page 77.

Nelson, Mac. *A Few Steps by Regular Teachers Can Help Substitutes with Class Instruction,* NASSP Bulletin, November 1983, pages 98–100.
- Advice of a substitute teacher to support effective substitute teaching.

Presberg, Helen. *Accept No Substitute (For Good Substitute Teaching),* Science and Children, September 1988, pages 26–28.

- Activities to help children develop their processing and inquiry skills with a Substitute Teacher. Illustrations with 25 kinds of skills.

Secor, Joan. *From a Substitute: I Am A 'Real Teacher,'* Instructor, August/September 1974, pages 134, 140, 142.
- A Substitute Teacher shares concerns about her day.

To A Substitute's School: Subs Are Part of A Team, Instructor, August/September 1974, page 138.
- School staff members should "plan ways to make substitutes more effective learning agents in the classroom." 10 suggestions.

For the Administrator

Clifton, Rodney A. *Survival in a Marginal Situation,* Urban Education, October 1987, pages 310–327.
- A study attempting to provide a simple explanation for the numerous problems that exist in substitute teaching. Suggests improvements.

Educational Resources Information Center (ERIC). A program of the National Library of Education, U.S. Department of Education. A nationwide information network designed to provide ready access to education literature. Web sites: www.ericsp.org and www.ericae.net.
Not Just a Warm Body: Changing Images of the Substitute Teacher, ERIC Digest, 1997, ED 412208, 9 references.

64

Substitute Teaching

Esposito, Frank J. *Improving the Role of Substitute Teachers,* NASSP Bulletin, December 1975, pages 47–50.
- Administrative planning as the key to improving the substitute teaching role.

Musso, Barbara Bonner. *Micro Resource Units Aid Substitute Teachers,* Educational Leadership, May 1970, pages 825–826.
- Training a corps of elementary Substitute Teachers and preparing study kits for classroom use.

Steltenpohl, Elizabeth H. *How to Uncomplicate Your Substitute Teacher Program and Make It Make Sense, Too,* American School Board Journal, February 1974, pages 37 and 56.
- Three steps to improve a district's Substitute Teacher program.

Tracey, Saundra J. *Improve Substitute Teaching with Staff Development,* NASSP Bulletin, May 1988, pages 85–88.
- Presents a staff development model: district and building links; classroom management and instruction; skill practice, feedback and refinement.

Warren, Harold. *A Program for Substitute Teachers,* School and Community, April 1970, page 14.
- A program for Substitute Teachers to produce "well oriented, full-time staff . . . acquainted with policies, procedures and academic programs."

Washington, Roosevelt, Jr. *Substitute Teachers Need Supervisory Help,* Educational Leadership, November 1972, pages 153–156.

Abdul-Haqq, Ismat. *Not Just a Warm Body: Changing Images of the Substitute Teacher,* ERIC Digest, September 1997, ED 412208, 4 pages, 9 references.

Grieder, Charles A. *The Role of the Substitute Teacher,* Education, April/May 1972, page 98.

Hartung, A. Bruce. *Substitute Teacher Policies: A National Inconsistency,* Contemporary Education, October 1972, pages 5–6.

65

McGerald, James. *Substitute Teachers: Seeking Meaningful Instruction in the Teacher's Absence,* Clearing House, September/October, 1994, pages 25–26.

Stevens, Thelma. *Wither the Substitute Teacher?,* Clearing House, December 1969, pages 229–231.

Wood, Linda L. and Thomas W. *Substitute: A Psychological Study,* Elementary School Journal, December 1974, pages 162–167.

Commercial Products

Cawthorne-Crafton, Barbara. *Instant Success for Classroom Teachers: New and Substitute Teachers Grades K Through 8,* Greenfield Publications, Scottsdale, AZ, ISBN 0-98066-60-5.

Collins S. Harold. *Classroom Management for Substitute Teachers,* ISBN 0-931993-03-2, *Mastering the Art of Substitute Teaching,* ISBN 0-931993-02-4, *Substitute Ingredients,* ISBN 0-931993-01-6, Garlic Press, Eugene, OR.

Freedman, Miriam and Teri Perl. *A Sourcebook for Substitutes and Other Teachers,* Addison-Wesley Publishing, Menlo Park, CA, ISBN 0-201006786-7

McMillan, Mary. *Lifesavers for Substitutes,* Good Apple, Torrance, CA, ISBN 0-86653-678-7.

Seeman, Cary and Shannon Hofstand. *Super Sub: A Must-Have Handbook for Substitute Teachers,* Addison-Wesley Longman, Inc, Reading, MA, ISBN 0-673363-80-5.

Smith, Geoffrey M., et al. *Substitute Teacher Handbook, Elementary K–8,* ISBN 1-890563-04-8, *Substitute Teacher Handbook, Secondary 9–12,* ISBN 1-890563-05-6, Utah State University, Substitute Teacher Training Institute, Logan, UT.